First Lost Tooth with Gabrielle

Nicole Gabor

Lerner Publications ◆ Minneapolis

Discover six early milestones alongside your favorite *Sesame Street* friends! From visiting the dentist to getting a library card, this series helps young children feel prepared for new and exciting experiences that are a part of growing up.

Sincerely,
The Editors at Sesame Workshop

Table of Contents

Baby Teeth.................. 4

Losing a Tooth 6

Types of Teeth 21
Glossary. 22
Read More 23
Index. 24

Baby Teeth

Baby teeth are teeth that start to grow in when we're babies. By the time you're three years old, you might have about twenty baby teeth.

How many baby teeth do you have?

Losing a Tooth

You may start to feel your first wiggly tooth when you're about five or six years old.

Losing your baby teeth is an exciting sign that you're growing.

Baby teeth get wiggly when grown-up teeth are underneath.

You may not see it, but there is a grown-up tooth that pushes the baby tooth out of the way.

A tooth that feels wiggly is called a loose tooth. Your loose tooth might feel wiggly when you touch it or brush your teeth.

You might be able to wiggle your loose tooth back and forth.

It can take a while for a loose tooth to fall out. A loose tooth can fall out at any time. It can fall out while you're in school or at home.

It could even fall out while you're eating your favorite snack!

After your baby tooth falls out, you might feel a hole in your gums where the tooth used to be. Gums are the soft, pink area that your teeth are attached to.

Soon a new tooth will start to grow in.

Your mouth might feel a little sore after you lose a tooth. This is because the grown-up tooth is pushing through your gums.

Before you know it, you'll have a grown-up tooth!

Whether you have baby teeth or grown-up teeth, it's important to take care of them. Do this by brushing your teeth twice a day and visiting the dentist.

Don't forget to brush your teeth in the morning and at night!

After all your baby teeth fall out, you'll have a whole new set of grown-up teeth.

Have you lost your first tooth yet?

Types of Teeth

Pointy or round, dull or sharp—teeth come in different shapes! Each tooth has its own job. There are four main types of teeth:

1. Incisors are front teeth to help you bite.
2. Canines are sharp, pointed teeth.
3. Premolars are behind canines.
4. Molars are strong teeth at the back of your mouth.

TYPES OF TEETH

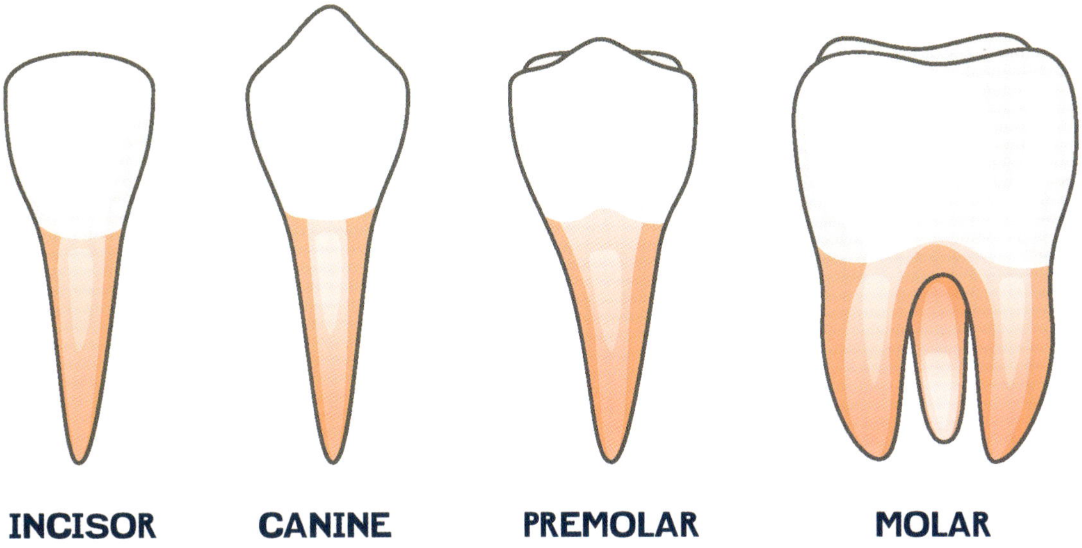

Glossary

baby teeth: your first set of teeth

dentist: a doctor who helps keep your teeth healthy

grown-up tooth: a tooth that grows in after losing a baby tooth

gums: the soft, pink area around your teeth

Read More

Cipriano, Jeri. *Going to the Dentist*. Egremont, MA: Red Chair, 2022.

Murray, Julie. *Tooth Types*. Minneapolis: Abdo Kids, 2024.

Sanderson, Whitney. *First Visit to the Dentist with Abby*. Minneapolis: Lerner Publications, 2026.

Photo Acknowledgments

Image credits: AJ_Watt/Getty Image, p. 3; Thomas Lai Yin Tang/Getty Images, p. 4; Cavan Images/Getty Images, pp. 7, 18; Igor Alecsander/Getty Images, p. 9; PeopleImages/Getty Images, p. 10; longoria-td/Getty Images, p. 12; Nina Buday/Shutterstock, p. 14; Ridofranz/Getty Images, p. 16; VectorMine/Shutterstock, p. 21. Design element: Agunar/Shutterstock.

Cover: Images By Tang Ming Tung/Getty Images.

Index

dentist, 18

grown-up tooth, 8–9, 16–18, 20

gums, 14, 16

loose tooth, 10–12

wiggly tooth, 6

Lerner Publications Company
An imprint of Lerner Publishing Group, Inc.
241 First Avenue North
Minneapolis, MN 55401 USA

For reading levels and more information, look up this title at www.lernerbooks.com.

Main body text set in MIkado.
Typeface provided by HvD Fonts.

Editor: Annie Zheng **Designer:** Mary Ross
Lerner team: Connie Kuhnz, Sue Marquis

Library of Congress Cataloging-in-Publication Data

Names: Gabor, Nicole, author.
Title: First lost tooth with Gabrielle / Nicole Gabor.
Description: Minneapolis : Lerner Publications, [2026] | Series: Sesame Street firsts | Includes bibliographical references and index. | Audience: Ages 4–8 | Audience: Grades K–1 | Summary: "The first lost tooth is an exciting time for kids! Young readers will love joining Gabrielle and her Sesame Street friends to learn what happens when they lose a tooth"— Provided by publisher.
Identifiers: LCCN 2024038539 (print) | LCCN 2024038540 (ebook) | ISBN 9798765661062 (lib. bdg.) | ISBN 9798765684849 (pbk) | ISBN 9798765680971 (epub)
Subjects: LCSH: Deciduous teeth—Juvenile literature. | Teeth—Juvenile literature. | Tooth loss—Juvenile literature.
Classification: LCC QP88.6 .G33 2026 (print) | LCC QP88.6 (ebook) | DDC 611/.314—dc23/eng/20250109

LC record available at https://lccn.loc.gov/2024038539
LC ebook record available at https://lccn.loc.gov/2024038540

Manufactured in the United States of America
1-1011811-53661-1/7/2025